MW00948335

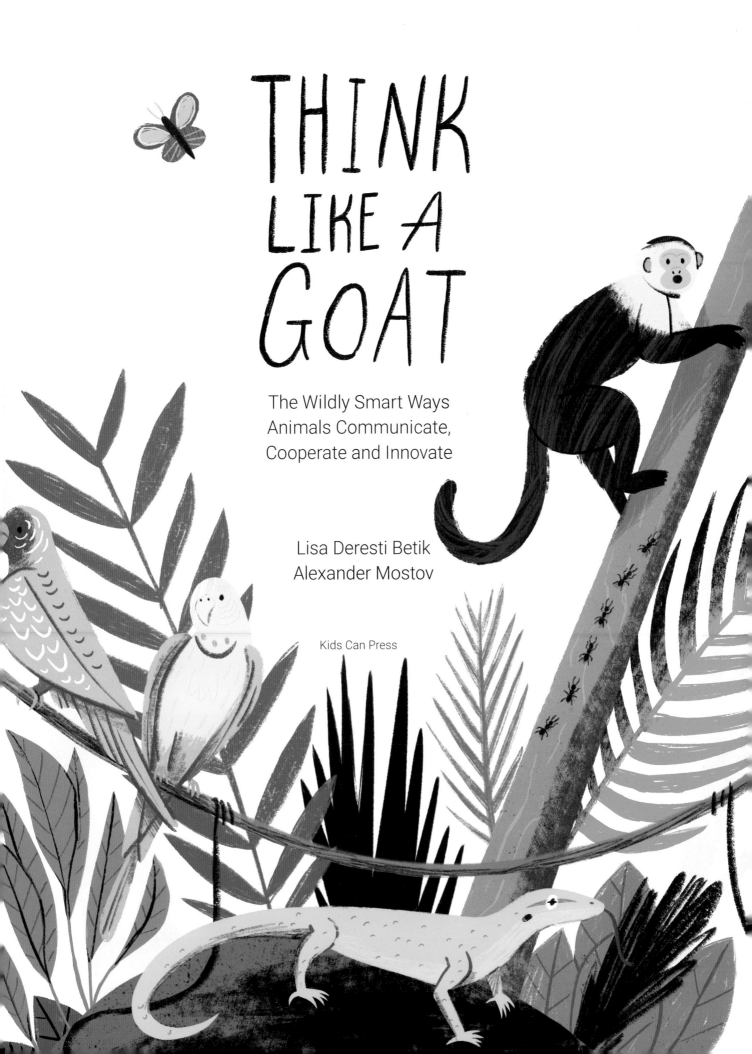

THINK LIKE A GOAT

The Wildly Smart Ways
Animals Communicate,
Cooperate and Innovate

Lisa Deresti Betik
Alexander Mostov

Kids Can Press

For my mom and dad, with love and thanks — L.D.B.
For all the animals in my life, especially my dog Dziga — A.M.

Acknowledgments

A team of really smart people made this book. I'm grateful to everyone at Kids Can Press whose talents and efforts helped bring these pages to life. Special thanks to my editor, Kathleen Keenan, for her insights and her sense of humor, and to Alexander Mostov for his amazing animal illustrations. Much appreciation to Dr. Frans de Waal and the many other scientists whose work on animals inspired this book. Love and thanks always to my family, my favorite partners in this wild life.

Text © 2023 Lisa Deresti Betik
Illustrations © 2023 Alexander Mostov

All rights reserved. No part of this publication may be reproduced, stored in a retrieval system or transmitted, in any form or by any means, without the prior written permission of Kids Can Press Ltd. or, in case of photocopying or other reprographic copying, a license from The Canadian Copyright Licensing Agency (Access Copyright). For an Access Copyright license, visit www.accesscopyright.ca or call toll free to 1-800-893-5777.

Many of the designations used by manufacturers and sellers to distinguish their products are claimed as trademarks. Where those designations appear in this book and Kids Can Press Ltd. was aware of a trademark claim, the designations have been printed in initial capital letters (e.g., Rubik's Cube).

Published in Canada and the U.S. by Kids Can Press Ltd.
25 Dockside Drive, Toronto, ON M5A 0B5

Kids Can Press is a Corus Entertainment Inc. company

www.kidscanpress.com

The artwork in this book was rendered digitally in Procreate.
The text is set in Roboto.

Edited by Kathleen Keenan
Designed by Marie Bartholomew

Printed and bound in Malaysia in 3/2023 by Times Offset

CM 23 0 9 8 7 6 5 4 3 2 1

Library and Archives Canada Cataloguing in Publication

Title: Think like a goat : the wildly smart ways animals communicate, cooperate and innovate / Lisa Deresti Betik ; Alexander Mostov.
Names: Deresti Betik, Lisa, 1972– author. | Mostov, Alexander, illustrator.
Description: Includes bibliographical references and index.
Identifiers: Canadiana (print) 20220456593 | Canadiana (ebook) 20220458545 | ISBN 9781525304552 (hardcover) | ISBN 9781525310706 (EPUB)
Subjects: LCSH: Animal behavior — Juvenile literature. | LCSH: Animal communication — Juvenile literature. | LCSH: Animal intelligence — Juvenile literature.
Classification: LCC QL751.5 .D47 2023 | DDC j591.5 — dc23

Kids Can Press gratefully acknowledges that the land on which our office is located is the traditional territory of many nations, including the Mississaugas of the Credit, the Anishnabeg, the Chippewa, the Haudenosaunee and the Wendat peoples, and is now home to many diverse First Nations, Inuit and Métis peoples.

We thank the Government of Ontario, through Ontario Creates; the Ontario Arts Council; the Canada Council for the Arts; and the Government of Canada for supporting our publishing activity.

TABLE *of* Contents

ALL KINDS *of Intelligence*

Humans are pretty smart. We learn at every stage of life, whether it's how to walk or how to run a business. We invent cool tools and systems (like scooters! backpacks! ice cream trucks! the internet!) to solve all sorts of problems. We use complicated languages to communicate with each other — hey, look! we're doing that right now in this book. We remember our past experiences and plan for future ones. It's no wonder we consider ourselves the most intelligent creatures on our planet. But ... are we, really?

Scientists who study animal behavior are asking us to think again. All kinds of animals have smarts that might surprise us. Did you know that an octopus can imitate a jellyfish, a sea snake or even a plant to avoid being eaten by predators? Chimpanzees use rocks and sticks as tools to help them crack open nuts and get termites out of logs.

Sparrows find their way to their winter homes even if they start 3700 km (2300 mi.) away from their normal flight route. Oh, and get this: crows recognize human faces, remember them for years and warn other crows about dangerous people! These and other fascinating discoveries are helping us understand that many creatures, from the tiny rock ant to the enormous blue whale, are more intelligent than we once believed.

To truly appreciate how smart other animals are, we shouldn't look at what they can do compared to us, but at how they've evolved to solve problems and survive in their own unique environments. Humans think and learn in impressive ways, for sure. But other creatures, with their different brains and special skills, have so many interesting things to teach us.

CHAPTER ONE

ALWAYS *Evolving*

*What do beetles, blue jays, porcupines and people all have in common? We're all connected to one another (and to every other thing that's ever lived!) through the processes of **evolution**.*

In the 1800s, naturalist and scientist Charles Darwin developed his theory that species change, or evolve, gradually, over many generations. Observing finches and other animals during his travels around the world, he noticed that there were small physical differences between creatures of the same species.

Darwin's Finches

A. geospiza magnirostris

B. geospiza parvula

C. geospiza fortis

D. geospiza olivacea

In the wild, animals of the same species compete for limited resources, such as food and space. Darwin realized that the animals with traits that give them a competitive advantage will survive and reproduce. Think of polar bears, which have thicker fur to protect them from the cold, or lizards that can change skin color to blend in with their surroundings. The surviving individual animals of a species pass these helpful traits on to their babies. Darwin called this process **natural selection**. A ground finch with a short, thick beak that's especially useful for crushing large seeds will have baby finches that also have short, thick beaks, and eventually those finches' babies will inherit short, thick beaks, too. In this way, helpful characteristics become more common in a species over time — a very long time. Continued gradual changes over many generations can eventually produce an entirely new species!

Parrot-like bill

Grasping bill

Probing bill

Crushing bill

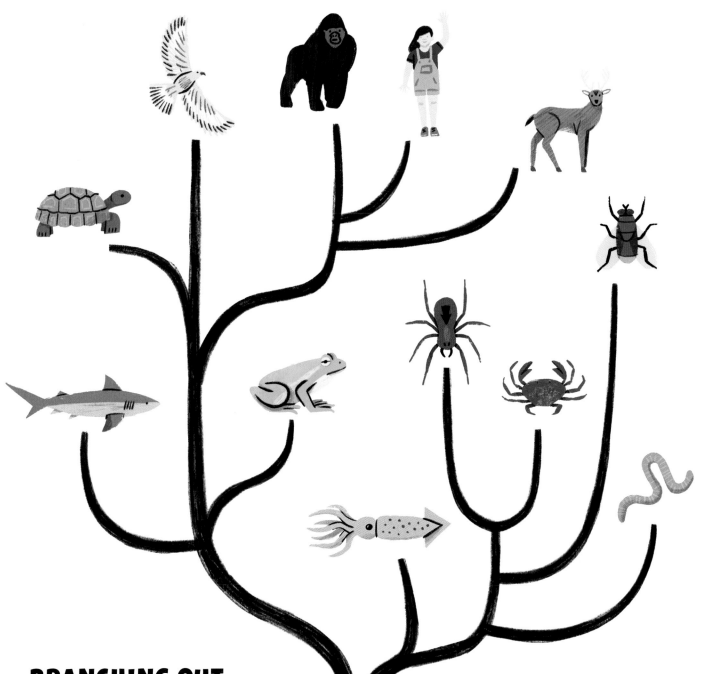

BRANCHING OUT

Over millions of years, evolution has created an astonishing variety of creatures on Earth, each with its own unique set of traits and abilities. Could you store thousands of individual seeds in lots of different places and then remember where they are six months later? Birds can. Would you think to carry shelter around with you so you could hide whenever you sense danger? Octopuses do. Many other animals also have special kinds of intelligence that make sense for the world they live in.

It's difficult to understand the behaviors of other animals, and humans are tempted to think that we've evolved to be the smartest of them all. But evolution is not like a ladder with humans at the top — it's more like a bushy tree. All species evolve in different directions as they learn to solve their own unique problems.

ANIMALS UP CLOSE

Ethologists study the behavior of animals in their natural environments. They look at how animals:

- communicate, compete and cooperate with one another

- find food, defend themselves and migrate to different places

- choose mates, reproduce and raise their young

- solve problems, learn and remember things

Ethologists also study the individual personalities of animals (yes, animals have personalities!), and how an animal's DNA and the size and structure of its brain influence how it behaves.

What is **personality**? It is the unique combination of behaviors, thoughts and feelings that makes you different from every other human. Personality exists in other animal species, too. No two fruit flies or squid or geese respond to their experiences in exactly the same way. You may have already noticed different animal personalities if you have two pugs or two tabby cats at home.

AN ELEPHANT AND A BANANA

The challenge for ethologists is to design studies that actually suit each species. They need to understand an animal's body and personality, along with how it senses things and what it's interested in, to really discover that animal's abilities.

A researcher might think an elephant that doesn't pick up a stick to get an out-of-reach banana doesn't understand how to use tools. But picking up a stick with its trunk blocks an elephant's nose, so it can't touch or smell the fruit. When the researcher offers a sturdy box instead, the elephant kicks the box over to the banana and stands on it to reach the prize. An elephant can use tools if the researcher gives it the right ones.

OPEN MINDS

With well-designed studies, scientists have been able to observe smart behaviors in all kinds of creatures. Animals can communicate with one another through calls or dances or even electric signals! They can cooperate with and learn from one another. They remember things and can solve problems using strategies and tools. Some animals even show signs of emotional intelligence — their behaviors suggest that they have **empathy** and play fairly. It's good to keep our own minds open as we learn more about other animals' amazing abilities. When we understand and respect other creatures, we can live more in harmony with them on our shared planet.

CHAPTER TWO

Critter COMMUNICATION

Have you ever wished your pets could talk to you? Nonhuman animals may not speak our languages (or know how to send a text!), but they've evolved to have their own ways of communicating. Animals use visual, auditory, tactile and chemical signals to share information with one another. They use their signals to tell where food is, warn of danger, defend their territories, organize group behavior and more.

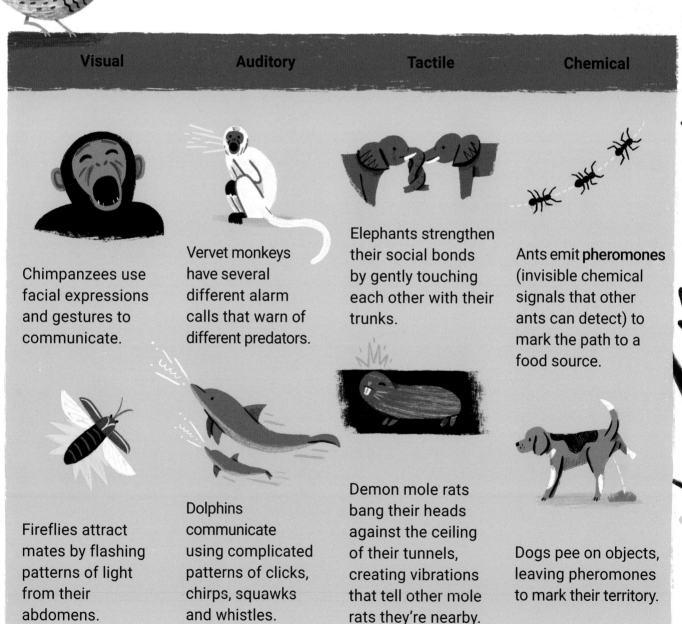

Visual	Auditory	Tactile	Chemical

Chimpanzees use facial expressions and gestures to communicate.

Vervet monkeys have several different alarm calls that warn of different predators.

Elephants strengthen their social bonds by gently touching each other with their trunks.

Ants emit **pheromones** (invisible chemical signals that other ants can detect) to mark the path to a food source.

Fireflies attract mates by flashing patterns of light from their abdomens.

Dolphins communicate using complicated patterns of clicks, chirps, squawks and whistles.

Demon mole rats bang their heads against the ceiling of their tunnels, creating vibrations that tell other mole rats they're nearby.

Dogs pee on objects, leaving pheromones to mark their territory.

LOOK, LISTEN, LEARN

Animal communication can involve a lot of complicated brain activity. For example, baby zebra finches know by **instinct** how to make the simple everyday calls of their species. But they *learn* how to sing more complex mating songs by listening to adult finches singing. Apes are born with an ability to use hand gestures to communicate, but the way they use these gestures can change. An ape can use a familiar gesture in a completely new way, and other apes in the group can learn this new behavior by copying it.

Research continues to uncover smart methods of communication in other animals, including parrots, ground squirrels, electric fish and more.

Squawk!

Pretty SMART!

MORE THAN A MIMIC

What are parrots famous for? Imitating what people say! But one African gray parrot named Alex showed that he was more than just a mimic. He could actually *understand* the meaning of the words he voiced.

Through his 30 years of training and practice with scientist Irene Pepperberg, Alex learned around a hundred labels for objects and could put them into categories. He understood colors, shapes, numbers and the concept of same/different. For example, Pepperberg would show Alex a green key and a green cup and ask "What's same?," and Alex could respond "Color." If she asked "What's different?," Alex could respond "Shape." He could also tell her whether an object was made of wool or paper or metal.

Alex's abilities — paying attention to the qualities of objects, understanding the questions he was asked, making judgments and giving the right answers — showed that parrots are pretty smart!

CHICKADEE-DEE-DEES

Ever notice the little black-capped birds that like to hang out in woods and backyards? They're chickadees, and they have a very sophisticated communication system. Their calls are made up of several distinct notes, which they can arrange in different ways to share information with other birds. Chickadees call to identify themselves, to tell where food is, to organize group movement and to warn of predators.

Chick-a-dee dee dee dee dee dee dee dee dee dee dee dee dee dee dee dee dee dee.

A chickadee calls a loud "*chick-a-dee*" when a predator is perched nearby. The number of "dees" added to the call gives other birds information about the size of the predator and how much of a threat it is. Smaller, quicker-flying (and therefore more dangerous!) predators, like the pygmy owl, get more "dees" (up to 23!). The chickadee's alarm call urges nearby birds to mob the predator and chase it away.

Chickadee calls are so informative and reliable that more than 50 different species pay attention to them. Nuthatches, jays and other birds will rush to mob a predator when they hear a chickadee sound the alarm.

ULTRASONIC SQUIRRELS?

Richardson's ground squirrels also call to warn of danger, making short, low-pitched chirps for flying predators and long, high-pitched whistles for threats on the ground. But sometimes ground squirrels open their mouths to call an alarm, and humans hear only a whisper. Wait... what? A whispering ground squirrel is producing an **ultrasonic** call, one that is so high-pitched that humans and many predators can't hear it. Ultrasonic calls let ground squirrels send top-secret warnings without giving away their location.

Ground squirrels don't consider all calls to be equally reliable, though. Scientists James Hare and Brent Atkins played recordings of different squirrels' alarm calls for young ground squirrels, while sometimes wheeling a scary stuffed badger toward them! The young squirrels learned to recognize which calls meant the badger was coming, and they eventually responded less to the other, unreliable ones. Smart!

HEADS AND TAILS

If you've ever thought your dog was trying to tell you something when it raised its eyebrows at you or showed you its tongue, you were probably right. Dogs use their bodies to signal to each other and to humans.

In dog-to-dog communication, a high tail shows confidence …

… while a low, tucked tail shows fear.

TAIL HIGH

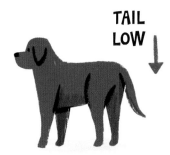

TAIL LOW

A tail wagging more to the right tells that a dog sees a situation as positive …

… and wagging to the left is negative.

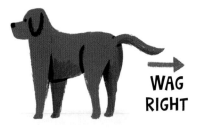

WAG RIGHT

WAG LEFT

A dog stares at another dog to threaten it …

… or avoids eye contact to lessen tension.

STARING

AVOIDING

Reading these and other body signals helps dogs understand and respond to one another's intentions and **emotions**.

OUR BEST FRIEND

Dogs have evolved to understand human signals, too, probably because they've lived closely with us for thousands of years. They read our body language and look where we look or point. They watch our faces and understand that eye contact means we're trying to communicate. Studies show dogs make more facial movements when humans are paying attention to them, and they'll keep signaling until we respond to them.

Cat people: your feline friends are good communicators, too! Adult cats don't usually meow at one another — they communicate through body language, touch, hisses and growls. But cats do meow at humans. Some domestic cats have learned to mix a high-pitched, urgent whine into their purr when they want food. The sound is similar to a crying human baby, and it's very hard to ignore.

ELECTRIC EXCHANGE

Here's a shocking example of animal communication: electric fish share information through electric signals! A specialized organ in their tail generates electric pulses that travel quickly in water. Other electric fish receive these signals through **electroreceptors** (groups of sensory cells) in their skin.

Each species of electric fish has its own unique signal, and individual fish can even change the rhythm and rate of theirs to communicate their personal identity and their mood.

What happens when electric fish with similar frequencies are in the same area? Each fish adjusts the frequency of its signal to avoid interference.

Electric fish aren't the only cool communicators. Other fish species send out information through **bioluminescence** (creating light through a chemical reaction in their bodies), grinding their teeth, rubbing their bones together, wiggling their fins or even farting! Canadian researcher Ben Wilson found that when herring gather together, they squeeze air bubbles out of their butts in distinct rhythms.

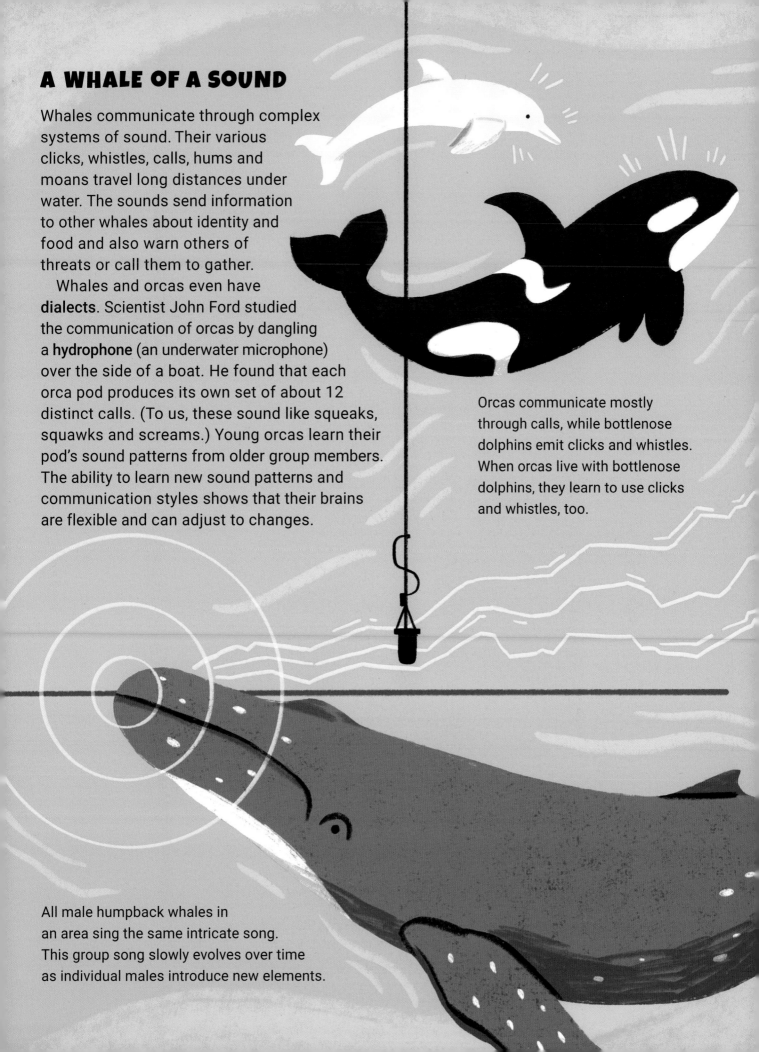

A WHALE OF A SOUND

Whales communicate through complex systems of sound. Their various clicks, whistles, calls, hums and moans travel long distances under water. The sounds send information to other whales about identity and food and also warn others of threats or call them to gather.

Whales and orcas even have **dialects**. Scientist John Ford studied the communication of orcas by dangling a **hydrophone** (an underwater microphone) over the side of a boat. He found that each orca pod produces its own set of about 12 distinct calls. (To us, these sound like squeaks, squawks and screams.) Young orcas learn their pod's sound patterns from older group members. The ability to learn new sound patterns and communication styles shows that their brains are flexible and can adjust to changes.

Orcas communicate mostly through calls, while bottlenose dolphins emit clicks and whistles. When orcas live with bottlenose dolphins, they learn to use clicks and whistles, too.

All male humpback whales in an area sing the same intricate song. This group song slowly evolves over time as individual males introduce new elements.

CHAPTER THREE

Better TOGETHER

How did you learn to make a sandwich? Tie your shoelaces? Play your favorite game? Chances are you learned these skills by watching other people do them. We live, work and play in groups at home, at school and everywhere else we go, and our interactions give us many chances to learn from one another.

Animals that live in groups also learn by observing and interacting with others. This is called *social learning*, and it can influence animals' decisions about their movement patterns, what they eat, how they avoid danger and more.

When a young sparrow has just left the nest, or a seal pup is being weaned from its mother, it has to learn quickly how to find good food and avoid predators. Watching and interacting with adults in the group lets young animals learn the solutions to these kinds of problems without having to go through lots of trial and error themselves.

JOINT EFFORT

Living in groups also gives animals opportunities to cooperate with one another. In many species, individuals work together so each of them can be better off. Have you ever shared your food with a hungry friend? Vampire bats do this, too — except their food is blood! They'll drink blood from horses, cows, pigs and birds and share it with other hungry bats to help their colony survive.

Researchers have even seen examples of cooperation between animals of different species. Coral groupers and moray eels hunt for reef fish together. Coyotes and badgers hunt together, too, combining their different strengths to catch more ground squirrels.

WHAT DO ANIMALS UNDERSTAND?

Some cooperative behaviors require certain smarts. In a study by Frans de Waal and other scientists, two elephants were presented with a heavy, out-of-reach food box, and the only way they could bring it closer was by pulling on ropes cooperatively. The elephants quickly learned not to even try pulling the ropes on their own — each one waited for another elephant to come and help. The elephants understood that they needed a partner if they wanted to get the food.

Cooperation and social learning allow animals to be more successful than they would be if they were all on their own.

TINY TEACHERS

Rock ants work together to build their nests in the cracks of rocks. They prefer dark, clean homes that have multiple small entrances and are big enough for the colony. If their home gets destroyed, the whole group moves to a suitable new one.

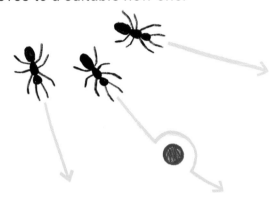

1. Experienced worker ants set out individually, learning **landmarks** along the way.

4. Each new ant will teach other ants, until a certain number of ants know the way.

2. Once a scout ant finds a good site, it returns home to teach the route to another worker ant.

5. All those ants will then carry the others to the new home. (It's faster than teaching every single ant!)

3. The scout ant only continues once the learning ant taps it from behind with its antennae.

6. The carried ants arrange things in the new home in the same way as the old one.

ANT ALGORITHMS

Ant colonies don't have a leader, so how do they manage to work together so well? Individual ants tend to follow **algorithms**, or specific sets of rules, when completing tasks. (You use algorithms when you follow a step-by-step process to solve a math problem or a Rubik's Cube.) The ants' algorithms are solutions they've learned over many generations of evolution. Algorithms help individual ants know just what to do so the whole colony can be successful.

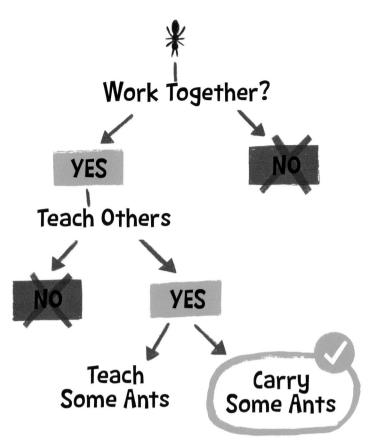

Work Together?

YES — NO

Teach Others

NO — YES

Teach Some Ants — Carry Some Ants

LEARN LIKE A LIZARD

Anna Wilkinson and other researchers were curious to know if lizards could learn through imitation. They showed videos to groups of lizards called bearded dragons, where a bearded dragon opened a gate to get to some tasty mealworms. When the lizards then had a chance to try it themselves, all of them were able to open the gate!

The bearded dragons imitated the exact behavior they saw: they used a sliding head movement to open the gate, and they opened it in the same direction, either right or left, as the bearded dragon in the video.

How did the researchers know that the lizards' behavior was the result of learning and not just instinct? They showed some bearded dragons a video with no bearded dragon in it, where the gate just opened by itself. When these bearded dragons were given a chance to try opening the gate, they didn't know what to do!

BUSINESS PARTNERS

They may be small, but cleaner wrasses have impressive social intelligence. They nibble parasites and dead skin off other fish, sometimes working on more than two thousand "clients" a day. Many of these clients are large predators that could easily eat a cleaner wrasse. But they don't, even when the cleaner wrasse swims into their mouths! This cooperation between species provides the cleaner wrasse with a meal and helps the other fish stay healthy.

Cleaner wrasses recognize whether their clients are local fish (those that stay in a small area and have only one cleaner nearby) or out-of-towners (those that travel farther and can choose between different cleaners). If a line forms, they will take care of the out-of-towners first and give them extra attention, since those fish could go somewhere else.

Sometimes a cleaner wrasse will cheat and bite off a tasty piece of healthy skin during a cleaning! But it's smart enough not to do this when other fish are watching, and never to out-of-town fish. The cleaner wrasse keeps up a good reputation so its clients will keep coming back.

THAT'S ACCURATE

Quick: there's a piece of popcorn whizzing through the air above you! Can you hit it by blasting a stream of water from your mouth?

Hmm, probably not. (It's much harder than you'd think. And don't blame this book if you get in trouble for trying!) But archerfish hunt for insects, spiders and small lizards this way — with incredible accuracy. Within milliseconds, an archerfish can calculate how far away the prey is, how much force is needed to strike it, where it will land and how fast to accelerate to grab it when it does.

Archerfish can learn how to hit a difficult target by watching another archerfish successfully do it. They don't even need to practice — just seeing the skilled fish repeatedly shoot accurate streams of water is enough. (It's like you watching Steph Curry shoot a bunch of three-pointers and then being able to shoot them yourself!) This learning from a distance suggests that archerfish can take the **viewpoint** of another fish. They see and understand the situation as the shooting archerfish does.

RAVENS REMEMBER

You've probably already heard about how smart ravens are — they're good at using tools and solving problems, and they can even plan for the future. In a Lund University study, researchers observed that ravens could choose and set aside a specific tool they knew would help them open a treat box. Scientists have also found that ravens can cooperate with other ravens. But these birds are picky about their work partners.

Remember the elephants and the rope-pulling test? Two ravens presented with the same problem can solve it without any training. They will pull on the ends of a rope at the same time to reach two pieces of cheese. But they're more likely to cooperate with a relative or friend, not just any old raven. And if one raven cheats and takes both pieces of cheese, the other raven remembers and usually refuses to cooperate with that raven in the future!

BOWERBIRD BUILDERS

Choosing a good partner is important to satin bowerbirds, too. Male bowerbirds learn to create brilliant **bowers** to attract a mate. They build two parallel arched walls and decorate the ground around them with a carefully arranged collection of objects: stones, flowers, feathers, berries, marbles, tiny human toys and other small treasures they find (or steal from other birds' bowers!). When a female bowerbird visits, the male performs an elaborate song and dance for her.

Female bowerbirds prefer males with impressive bowers who are good at singing and dancing. Scientists think these skills might tell her that the male is artistic, athletic and a good learner — important qualities in a mate.

Male bowerbirds are not born with all of the skills needed to impress a female — they have to develop them. Young males spend a lot of time watching older ones build bowers. They also role-play while visiting older males' bowers. These actions are good for both birds: the young male gets to observe how the older one sings and dances, and the older male gets a chance to practice.

MEERKAT MENTORS

Did you know that wild meerkats eat insect larvae, centipedes, lizards, small mammals and … SCORPIONS?! Clearly those scorpions are dangerous and difficult to catch. But meerkat pups don't have to figure out how to hunt all on their own. Adults in the group teach them, by gradually giving them more advanced lessons in how to manage poisonous prey.

Adult meerkats stay near the pups and watch while they learn to handle prey. They'll nudge lizards or scorpions with their nose or paws to encourage the pups to eat. And if prey escapes a pup's grip, the adults will catch it again and make it weaker so the pup can try again.

Meerkat mentoring is a kind of cooperation: experienced adults actively change their behavior to help pups learn the survival skills they need.

First: An adult kills a scorpion before giving it to the pup to eat.

Next: An adult bites off a live scorpion's stinger, then lets the pup practice handling it.

Eventually: An adult brings the pup a whole live scorpion to catch. Now, the pup will be ready to hunt for itself!

WHOM TO GROOM?

Ever brushed or braided a friend's hair? Sooty mangabeys do something similar — they pick through each other's hair to remove dirt and pests. This grooming helps keep the monkeys physically healthy, but it's also an important cooperative behavior. A monkey can trade a grooming session for favors from another monkey, such as backup during a fight or food after a hunt.

Researcher Alexander Mielke and his team have observed that sooty mangabeys use information about others in their group to choose the best grooming partner (kind of like when you know a classmate has candy, so you do her a favor, hoping she'll share with you at recess). The monkeys usually choose to groom their friends, mothers with babies and higher-ranked individuals (ones that win fights and have the best access to food and mates). Sooty mangabeys also make sure not to choose partners whose close friends are nearby. Partners with friends in the audience might be interrupted, or they might even leave early to go groom their friends instead!

All this grooming behavior is smart: sooty mangabeys cooperate with individuals that will benefit them the most, without wasting their time or energy.

CHAPTER FOUR

Problem SOLVED

Life in the wild can be dangerous! To survive, animals must navigate, find food and shelter, avoid predators and more. Solving these problems requires serious brainpower.

MENTAL MAPPING

When you ride your bike to your friend's house, you're using a **cognitive map**. You have a mental representation of your surroundings that helps you know how far and in which direction you should go. Other animals use cognitive maps, too. Rats do, to efficiently find a food treat in a maze experiment. Honeybees use mental maps to find their way to food and nesting sites.

THERE'S A TOOL FOR THAT

Some animals solve problems with tools. Female bottlenose dolphins protect their **rostrums** (beaks) against sharp rocks by placing sea sponges over them while fishing. New Caledonian crows use sticks to get out-of-reach food and can even combine several to make a longer stick.

While some tool-using behaviors appear to be instinctive, others are learned. It's a sign of intelligence when animals can use tools flexibly to solve new problems. (Imagine you're really hungry while doing your homework. If you pile books on the floor and use them to get cookies from a high shelf, you're using tools flexibly!)

REMEMBER WHEN ...

Some animals are capable of **episodic-like memory**: they can remember the what, where and when of their past experiences. Orangutans who are returned to the same room with the same researcher and the same problem after three years can remember where to find the right tool to reach some bananas.

Animals with episodic-like memory seem to use memories of their past to help guide their actions in the present. (If you fall off your book pile and remember to use a chair next time, you're doing the same.)

Ever been stuck on a problem (like how to keep your siblings out of your room?), and suddenly a new solution just pops into your head? These light bulb moments are called **insightful problem-solving**, and other animals have them, too. Instead of using trial and error (trying different methods until they find a solution), animals such as elephants, crows and chimpanzees seem to have an "aha!" moment: a flash of sudden insight as their brains connect pieces of information.

HUNGRY HUNGRY HUMMINGBIRDS

A hummingbird beats its tiny wings an incredible 70 times per second! These high-energy little birds need to eat every 10 minutes — they visit hundreds of flowers in their territory multiple times each day to get nectar. Remembering the exact locations of all those flowers matters, as hummingbirds can't afford to waste time or energy searching for food.

Hummingbirds can remember where a flower is after visiting it only once for a few seconds. They even keep track of which flowers have the most nutritious food and how long each flower takes to fill up again with nectar. This isn't easy, since different flowers refill at different rates. A hummingbird will only come back to flowers after enough time has passed. Amazing!

How do hummingbirds remember all these details? Scientists Susan Healy and Andrew Hurly wondered if the birds might use a flower's color as a clue. But they discovered that hummingbirds seem to form mental maps of the position of each flower in their territory.

The two scientists provided rufous hummingbirds with different-colored cardboard flowers filled with tasty sugar solutions and refilled them at different rates. When the hummingbirds were choosing flowers to feed from, they seemed to ignore any color clues and focused instead on the layout of the flower field.

In one study, Dr. Healy moved the flowers 20 cm (8 in.) to 50 cm (20 in.) away from their original spots. When the hummingbirds returned and the flowers weren't where they expected them to be, they just flew away!

QUITE A CACHE

Remembering where you stored your cereal or chocolate milk is pretty simple — it's either in a cupboard or the fridge. But western scrub jays must remember thousands of different places where they've hidden fruit, nuts, seeds, insects and worms.

Scrub jays remember not only where their food **caches** are, but also which items they stored there and when. Their memory helps them to recover easily spoiled foods (worms, bugs and berries) before they rot, saving the longer-lasting nuts and seeds.

Scrub jays often steal one another's caches, so these birds also keep track of who is watching them. A jay being watched by a rival is more likely to go back and move the food later. (Or it might just pretend to move the food while the other bird is watching!)

REPTILES GET A BAD RAP

For a long time, scientists mostly ignored reptiles in their animal intelligence research. Lizards, turtles and snakes had a reputation for being not very bright after they performed poorly on some cognitive tests in the 1960s. But surprising recent studies have shown that these cold-blooded creatures are much smarter than we once thought.

Anoles (tropical lizards) typically catch moving prey by darting at it from above. But when scientists Manuel Leal and Brian Powell put them in a situation where this strategy wouldn't work, the lizards came up with new methods.

The researchers hid insect larvae in small holes covered with tight-fitting blue caps.

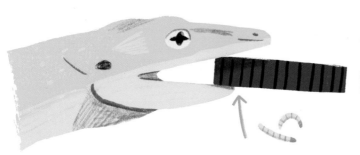

Some of the lizards discovered they could lift the lids by biting them from the side.

Some lizards used their noses to bump the caps off from underneath.

Using their noses or biting things from the side are unusual ways for anoles to get food — they don't typically do these things in the wild.

These anoles showed that they can learn new behaviors to solve an unusual problem.

A-MAZE-ING TORTOISES

A red-footed tortoise named Moses showed her smarts in an eight-arm radial maze like the one below.

The end of each arm held a piece of strawberry. Moses was placed in the center and given eight chances to get the treats. She quickly learned to navigate the maze so that she didn't go back to any arm where she'd already eaten the strawberry.

Moses seemed to form a mental map to navigate, using objects she could see beyond the maze as **landmarks** to help her remember where she'd been. When scientist Anna Wilkinson put a black curtain around the maze and hid those landmarks, Moses came up with another plan to snatch the strawberries: she always visited the maze arm next to the one she'd just left, until she'd been to them all.

Scientists now know that cognitive tests involving lizards, turtles and other cold-blooded creatures need to be done in a room that's warm, like their natural environment. Cold temperatures make reptiles sluggish and less likely to demonstrate their true abilities.

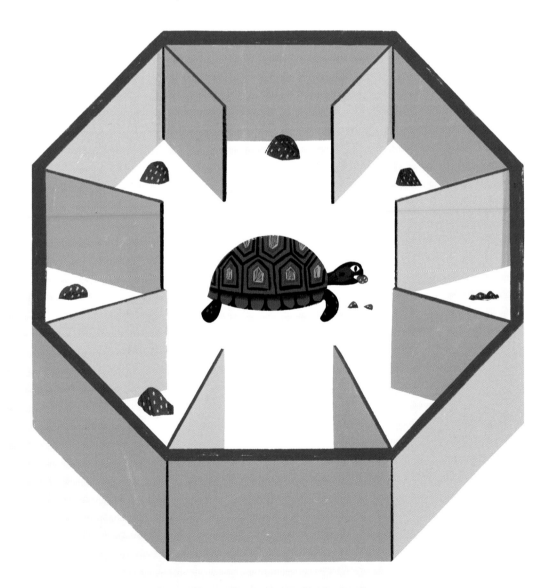

THE GOAT

If you've ever visited a farm, you may have been entertained by goats climbing and pigs rolling in mud. Would it surprise you to hear that these animals are skilled problem solvers with excellent memories?

In one study at Queen Mary University of London, goats were given a two-step puzzle-solving challenge. To get a tasty piece of fruit out of a box, they had to pull on a rope with their teeth to activate a lever, and then lift the lever up with their snout. Nine of the 12 goats in the study could solve this puzzle after four tries. (Two other goats tried to use their horns to force the box open, so they were disqualified!)

When the scientists presented these nine goats with the same puzzle 10 months later, all remembered how to get the fruit in less than two minutes.

Goats are not the silly, garbage-eating creatures many people think they are. Their long life span — 15 to 18 years — allows them to develop lots of skills and memories (and they're actually picky eaters who are good at finding the best blade of grass).

A PIG'S PERSPECTIVE

Pigs are very intelligent animals. In mazes that test their **spatial abilities**, pigs are quick to learn and remember where food is located. They can also remember which food site had more food and will choose to return to that one later.

One study showed that pigs also use other pigs' knowledge to their advantage when solving a problem — and may even develop strategies to trick other pigs!

This **strategic** behavior suggests that pigs may be able to see things from the perspective of other pigs.

1. Two pigs enter an arena together. The smaller pig already knows where food is hidden. The larger pig knows there's food, but not where it is.

2. The smaller pig goes straight to the food. The larger pig searches randomly at first … but then sees that the smaller pig knows something useful. The big pig follows the small one and takes most of the food.

3. Next time, the smaller pig starts going to the food site only when the larger pig isn't watching.

SEA OTTERS ROCK

Sea otters are strategic, too — they can use tools to get at tough-to-crack food. Some will smash their thick-shelled prey, such as snails and clams, against large rocks or on smaller rocks that they balance on their stomachs. Sometimes they tuck a rock in their armpit so they can reuse it later.

All sea otters seem to be born with an instinct for using tools. But expertly using a rock to smash open prey takes learning and practice, and not every sea otter develops this skill. Sea otters living in groups that eat more thick-shelled foods are more likely to learn, by watching their mothers do it.

Sea otters that use tools don't use them every time they find prey. This is a sign of flexible behavior — it suggests an otter decides whether or not a tool is right for a particular situation.

Scientists have noticed that when sea otters are cracking shells against rocks, they usually place their right paw slightly on top. It's possible that sea otters have a preferred "hand," like we do.

OH! OCTOPUS

An octopus is a marvel. These sea creatures have a complex nervous system that includes a large central brain, plus millions of **neurons** distributed among their eight tentacles. Each arm can "think" for itself and act on its own!

Octopuses are curious creatures with individual personalities. They explore, solve problems, play and even plan for future events.

Octopuses can quickly change their shape, color and movement to camouflage themselves as rocks, plants or other sea creatures.

They gather empty coconut shells to build shelters.

They carry the shells around in case they need to hide from predators.

They recognize and react differently to individual humans.

They create mental maps and can remember information about places they've been.

They repeatedly blow water jets at bottles placed in their tanks, apparently just for fun!

They're difficult to keep in aquariums because they take things apart!

They can open jar lids to get crabs out.

CHAPTER FIVE

MIXED *Emotions*

Your dog certainly looks happy when you play with him or give her a treat. But do nonhuman animals really have feelings? It's harder to answer this than you might think. Scientists can't study animal emotions directly — they can't ask an animal how it feels or get inside its mind to understand what it's experiencing. But an animal's body responses and behaviors — its posture, facial expressions, movements and sounds — are all clues that allow scientists to infer what it's feeling. Current research suggests that many different animals experience fear, joy, anger, compassion, grief and more. These behaviors are signs to scientists that other animal species have emotions, too.

Wolves show signs of happiness — tail-wagging, whining, jumping — when they see each other after being apart.

Younger female chimpanzees collect water in their mouths to bring to an old female who can't move well, showing what seems to be concern for her well-being.

Magpies lay grass beside the body of a dead bird and stand by for a few moments before flying away, in what may be a show of mourning.

Elephants seem to soothe one another in stressful situations through chirping and gentle touching with their trunks.

When dogs watch their caregivers give food to another dog, their brains light up in the same area that a jealous human's brain does.

CONTAGIOUS CONNECTIONS

Have you ever noticed you have an urge to yawn when you see another person yawning? This is called **yawn contagion**, and some other animals, including chimpanzees, dogs and budgies, also demonstrate it. Both in humans and in other animals, yawn contagion may be related to **empathy** (the ability to understand how others are feeling and to share those feelings).

Many scientists now believe (as Darwin did) that emotions are not just a human experience. They exist throughout the animal kingdom, because they serve a useful purpose. Emotions help all kinds of animals figure out the best response in any given situation and improve their chances of survival.

RAVEN REACTIONS

Animals living in groups sometimes fight over food or territory or ranking (kind of like you arguing with your siblings about who gets the last granola bar!). But they also appear to comfort and make up with one another after conflicts to keep their relationships in good shape.

University of Vienna scientists observed ravens for two years. They noticed that after fights, many bystander ravens (especially relatives and "friends") appeared to soothe the victim by sitting close by, touching it and straightening its feathers. The ravens seemed to be responding with empathy to the emotions of the victim.

In another study, Jessie Adriaense and other researchers placed two ravens in side-by-side compartments. They showed one of the ravens two boxes, one containing raw carrots and one containing dried dog food, and then took one of the boxes away. The second raven watched the first raven's reactions. Ravens much prefer dog food, so the ones that were left with carrots just ignored the food and scratched at the ground. Then the researchers gave the watching raven a box that might contain food. The ravens that had seen their partner react negatively showed less interest in the box. It appeared they were matching the emotions of the other raven.

SECOND CHOICE: CHOCOLATE

Rats seem to have empathy, too. In a Kwansei Gakuin University study, two rats were placed inside a box, in separate compartments divided by a see-through wall. One rat's compartment was dry, while the other rat had to swim in water (which rats really don't like). The wet rat could only escape the water if the dry rat opened one of two doors in the wall. The other door wouldn't help the wet rat, but would allow the dry rat to get one of its favorite treats — chocolate!

Most of the time, the dry rats chose to open the helpful door before opening the chocolate door. And rats that had been in the wet compartment themselves were the fastest to help. It was as if their own negative memories motivated them to rescue the other rat.

A study by Shimpei Ishiyama and Michael Brecht suggests that rats experience pleasure when they're tickled on their backs or their bellies. They make ultrasonic giggle-like squeaks and do "joy jumps" in the air!

MONKEY BUSINESS

What would happen if everybody in your family got a bigger piece of cake than you did? You'd be thinking, "Hey, no fair," right? A study by Sarah Brosnan and Frans de Waal showed that capuchin monkeys also seem to know when something's not fair.

Two monkeys learned that they could get a food reward by passing the researcher a pebble.

When both monkeys were given a piece of cucumber as the reward, they each took the food and kept passing pebbles to the researcher.

But when one monkey was given cucumber and one received a much-preferred grape, the first monkey banged its hands on the floor and threw the piece of cucumber at the researcher!

This behavior suggests that capuchin monkeys have an understanding of social rules — they know there are "right" and "wrong" behaviors and ways to be treated. Scientists think this understanding is one of the building blocks of **morality** in humans.

CARING CHIMPANZEES

Can you guess what happened when pairs of chimpanzees were given the same cucumber-grape test as the capuchin monkeys? Some of the chimpanzees actually tried to make things equal by refusing the grape until their partner got one, too.

In an Emory University study, chimpanzees could choose one of two different-colored tokens to exchange with a researcher.

One color would earn the chimpanzee a food reward. The other color would earn a food reward for that chimpanzee and for another chimpanzee. Even though the token-exchanging chimpanzees would get a reward no matter which token they chose, they more often chose the token that also helped their partner. Their unselfish choices suggest that chimpanzees have concern for others' well-being.

HUGS AND KISSES

Chimpanzees' behavior after fights also suggests they have empathy. Bystanders try to comfort victims, and aggressors and victims make up with one another through hugs, kisses and grooming. Like humans, chimpanzees have individual personalities and show different levels of concern for others. Some chimpanzees are much more likely than others to offer comfort to their fellow apes.

ELEPHANT BONDS

Comfort, our natural response to loss, helps humans when we're grieving. **Anthropologist** Barbara J. King thinks other animals may experience grief, too. Their behavior changes when an individual they know dies. Like humans, they might eat or sleep less, become withdrawn or show emotional stress through their body language and the sounds they make.

Field observations of elephants tell us that when an elephant dies, other elephants react to its body. They gently explore it with their trunks and feet. They may rock it back and forth, or try to lift or pull it while showing signs of distress. Some elephants will return several times over the days following the death and will show interest in the bones (especially the skulls and tusks) for years afterwards.

Elephants live in groups and form close, long-lasting bonds with other elephants — they recognize and remember individuals. They often touch each other's tusks with their trunks as part of their social behavior. When an elephant dies, touching the tusks and body seems to allow other elephants to identify it. Is an elephant experiencing grief when it reacts this way? Scientists are still exploring what it means, but grief is a real possibility.

A GREATER UNDERSTANDING

Whether it's showing strong social bonds, moving to a new home, sounding an alarm call, using tools or remembering exactly where to find hidden food, animal behavior shows us there's definitely more than one way to be intelligent. Animals have evolved to be smart in ways that help them survive and thrive in their own environments. Humans are only beginning to understand them.

Animals communicate with one another, using scents, sounds and other signals to share information. They teach and learn from one another and cooperate so that each of them is better off. They have memories and solve all sorts of problems. They use what they know from their past to help them figure out what to do in the present. They even seem to experience emotions, from joy to empathy to grief.

Knowing this, what will you see now when you look at a bear, a bat or a bumblebee? Scientists hope we'll realize the world is full of super-smart creatures, and there is still so much for us to learn from them.

GLOSSARY

algorithm: a step-by-step process or set of rules for solving a problem

anthropologist: a scientist who studies the biology, culture and relationships of humans and their ancestors

bioluminescence: light created and given off by living things through chemical reactions in their bodies

bower: an arched structure the male bowerbird builds out of twigs and grasses and decorates with brightly colored objects to impress a female

cache: food that an animal has hidden away to eat later

cognitive map: a mental representation of an individual's surroundings

dialect: a particular group's way of speaking a language

electroreceptors: groups of very sensitive sensory cells in the skin of electric fish that receive electric signals from other fish

emotions: complex mental states and physical changes in the body in response to experiences

empathy: the ability to understand how others are feeling and to share those feelings

episodic-like memory: nonhuman animals' ability to remember the what, where and when of their past experiences

ethologist: a scientist who studies the behavior of animals in their natural environments

evolution: the theory that all living things have grown and developed from earlier organisms. Over time, the genetic traits of a species gradually change through the process of natural selection, eventually producing entirely new species.

hydrophone: an underwater microphone used for listening to and recording ocean sounds

insightful problem-solving: arriving at the solution to a problem in a sudden flash of understanding

instinct: a natural tendency to behave or react in a particular way

landmark: an easily seen and recognized object on land

morality: a system of beliefs about what is right and wrong or about what are good and bad behaviors

natural selection: the process by which species become better suited to their environments over time. Organisms with physical traits that give them an advantage over others in their species will survive, reproduce and pass their helpful traits on to the next generation.

neurons: microscopic cells in the nervous system that communicate with one another through electrical and chemical signals

personality: the unique combination of behaviors, thoughts and feelings that makes you different from every other human

pheromones: invisible chemical signals given off by an animal

rostrum: the long snout, or beak, of a dolphin

social learning: learning that happens through interacting with others and watching their behaviors

spatial abilities: the ability to understand and remember where an object is located in relation to other objects

strategic: carefully designed or planned to achieve a specific goal

ultrasonic: having sound waves with higher frequencies than human ears can hear

viewpoint: a position or perspective from which an individual sees or understands something

yawn contagion: the tendency for individuals to have an urge to yawn when they see others yawning

SELECTED SOURCES

Ackerman, Jennifer. *The Genius of Birds*. Penguin Press, 2016.

Boysen, Dr. Sally, and Dr. Deborah Custance. *The Smartest Animals on the Planet*. Firefly Books Ltd., 2009.

Keim, Brandon. "The Intriguing New Science That Could Change Your Mind about Rats." *Wired*, 28 January 2015. www.wired.com/2015/01/reconsider-the-rat/.

McGowan, Kat. "Of Beasts and Brainpower." *Popular Science*, Spring 2018, pp. 58–63.

"Moral Behavior in Animals – Frans de Waal." *TED*, November 2011. https://www.ted.com/talks/frans_de_waal_moral_behavior_in_animals.

Morell, Virginia. *Animal Wise: The Thoughts and Emotions of Our Fellow Creatures*. Crown Publishers, 2013.

"Mysteries of the Animal Mind." *The Nature of Things* season 51, episode 11. Merit Motion Pictures and the Canadian Broadcasting Corporation, 2012.

Nuwer, Rachel. "Fish Have Feelings, Too." *PBS Nova*, 4 September 2018. www.pbs.org/wgbh/nova/article/fish-have-feelings-too/.

"Think Like An Animal." *The Nature of Things* season 56, episode 7. Written and directed by Leora Eisen, 90th Parallel Productions Ltd. and the Canadian Broadcasting Corporation, 2016.

Waal, F.B.M. de. *Are We Smart Enough to Know How Smart Animals Are?* W.W. Norton & Company, 2017.

INDEX